50 30-Minute Meal Recipes for Home

By: Kelly Johnson

Table of Contents

- Quick and Easy Chicken Stir-Fry
- Spaghetti Aglio e Olio with Cherry Tomatoes
- Lemon Garlic Shrimp Pasta
- Caprese Avocado Salad with Balsamic Glaze
- Mediterranean Chickpea Salad
- Teriyaki Salmon with Broccoli
- Taco Stuffed Bell Peppers
- Pesto Chicken Quesadillas
- Sesame Ginger Beef and Vegetable Stir-Fry
- One-Pan Lemon Herb Chicken with Veggies
- Shrimp and Asparagus Stir-Fry
- Cajun Chicken Pasta
- Caprese Chicken Skillet
- Vegetarian Black Bean and Corn Quesadillas
- Honey Garlic Glazed Salmon
- Mushroom and Spinach Risotto
- Buffalo Chicken Lettuce Wraps
- Easy Beef and Broccoli
- Lemon Butter Garlic Shrimp
- Margherita Flatbread Pizza
- Chicken Piccata with Lemon Caper Sauce
- Zucchini Noodles with Pesto and Cherry Tomatoes
- Quick and Healthy Turkey Chili
- Garlic Parmesan Crusted Tilapia
- Thai Basil Chicken Stir-Fry
- Mango Salsa Chicken Bowls
- Mushroom and Spinach Quesadillas
- Teriyaki Tofu Stir-Fry
- Crispy Baked Lemon Garlic Chicken Thighs
- Shrimp Scampi with Linguine
- Tomato Basil Grilled Cheese Sandwiches
- Lemon Herb Quinoa Salad
- BBQ Chicken Salad with Avocado
- Crispy Fish Tacos with Cabbage Slaw
- Pesto Zoodle Bowl with Grilled Chicken

- Mongolian Beef Skillet
- Caprese Stuffed Chicken Breast
- Quick and Easy Margherita Pasta
- Lemon Dill Salmon Cakes
- Mushroom and Goat Cheese Omelette
- Sesame Orange Chicken Lettuce Wraps
- Crispy Chickpea and Avocado Wrap
- Shrimp and Broccoli Alfredo
- Southwest Quinoa Bowl
- Sheet Pan Fajitas with Chicken
- Greek Chicken Souvlaki
- Cilantro Lime Shrimp Tacos
- Pasta Primavera with Lemon Parmesan Sauce
- Caprese Quinoa Salad
- Quick and Easy Beef Burrito Bowl

Quick and Easy Chicken Stir-Fry

Ingredients:

- 1 lb (450g) boneless, skinless chicken breasts, thinly sliced
- 2 tablespoons soy sauce
- 1 tablespoon oyster sauce
- 1 tablespoon hoisin sauce
- 1 tablespoon cornstarch
- 2 tablespoons vegetable oil, divided
- 3 cups mixed vegetables (broccoli, bell peppers, snap peas, carrots), chopped
- 3 cloves garlic, minced
- 1 tablespoon ginger, grated
- 2 green onions, sliced
- Sesame seeds (optional, for garnish)
- Cooked rice or noodles, for serving

Instructions:

Prepare the Chicken:
- In a bowl, combine the sliced chicken with soy sauce, oyster sauce, hoisin sauce, and cornstarch. Mix well and let it marinate for 10-15 minutes.

Stir-Fry Chicken:
- Heat 1 tablespoon of vegetable oil in a wok or large skillet over medium-high heat. Add the marinated chicken and stir-fry for 3-4 minutes or until cooked through. Remove the chicken from the pan and set aside.

Cook Vegetables:
- In the same pan, add another tablespoon of oil. Add the minced garlic, grated ginger, and mixed vegetables. Stir-fry for 4-5 minutes until the vegetables are tender-crisp.

Combine and Finish:
- Return the cooked chicken to the pan with the vegetables. Toss everything together until well combined and heated through.

Garnish and Serve:
- Garnish the stir-fry with sliced green onions and sesame seeds if desired. Serve the quick and easy chicken stir-fry over cooked rice or noodles.

Enjoy this flavorful and speedy chicken stir-fry that's perfect for busy weeknights. Feel free to customize the vegetables and adjust the sauce according to your preferences.

Spaghetti Aglio e Olio with Cherry Tomatoes

Ingredients:

- 8 oz (225g) spaghetti
- 4 tablespoons extra-virgin olive oil
- 4 cloves garlic, thinly sliced
- 1/2 teaspoon red pepper flakes (adjust to taste)
- 1 pint (about 2 cups) cherry tomatoes, halved
- Salt and black pepper, to taste
- Fresh parsley, chopped, for garnish
- Grated Parmesan cheese, for serving

Instructions:

Cook the Spaghetti:
- Cook the spaghetti in a large pot of salted boiling water according to the package instructions until al dente. Reserve about 1/2 cup of pasta water before draining.

Prepare the Sauce:
- While the pasta is cooking, heat the olive oil in a large skillet over medium heat. Add the sliced garlic and red pepper flakes. Sauté for about 1-2 minutes or until the garlic is golden and fragrant.

Add Cherry Tomatoes:
- Add the halved cherry tomatoes to the skillet. Cook for 2-3 minutes, just until the tomatoes start to soften. Season with salt and black pepper to taste.

Combine with Spaghetti:
- Add the cooked and drained spaghetti directly to the skillet. Toss everything together, ensuring the pasta is well-coated with the garlic and olive oil mixture. If the pasta seems dry, add a bit of the reserved pasta water to loosen it up.

Garnish and Serve:
- Garnish the Spaghetti Aglio e Olio with chopped fresh parsley. Serve immediately with grated Parmesan cheese on the side.

Enjoy this quick and flavorful pasta dish that highlights the simplicity of quality ingredients. The addition of cherry tomatoes adds a burst of sweetness to complement the garlicky olive oil sauce.

Lemon Garlic Shrimp Pasta

Ingredients:

- 8 oz (225g) linguine or spaghetti
- 1 lb (450g) large shrimp, peeled and deveined
- Salt and black pepper, to taste
- 4 tablespoons unsalted butter
- 4 cloves garlic, minced
- 1/2 teaspoon red pepper flakes (optional, for heat)
- Zest of 1 lemon
- Juice of 1 lemon
- 1/4 cup fresh parsley, chopped
- Grated Parmesan cheese, for serving

Instructions:

Cook the Pasta:
- Cook the linguine or spaghetti in a large pot of salted boiling water according to the package instructions until al dente. Reserve about 1/2 cup of pasta water before draining.

Season and Cook Shrimp:
- Season the shrimp with salt and black pepper. In a large skillet, melt 2 tablespoons of butter over medium-high heat. Add the shrimp and cook for 2-3 minutes per side or until they are opaque and cooked through. Remove the shrimp from the skillet and set aside.

Prepare the Lemon Garlic Sauce:
- In the same skillet, add the remaining 2 tablespoons of butter. Add minced garlic and red pepper flakes (if using). Sauté for about 1-2 minutes until the garlic is fragrant.

Combine with Pasta:
- Add the cooked and drained pasta directly to the skillet with the garlic butter. Toss to coat the pasta with the flavorful mixture. If the pasta seems dry, add a bit of the reserved pasta water.

Add Lemon and Shrimp:
- Add the lemon zest, lemon juice, and cooked shrimp to the pasta. Toss everything together until well combined and heated through.

Garnish and Serve:
- Garnish the Lemon Garlic Shrimp Pasta with chopped fresh parsley. Serve immediately with grated Parmesan cheese on the side.

Enjoy this light and refreshing pasta dish with succulent shrimp, brightened up by the flavors of lemon and garlic. It's a perfect option for a quick and flavorful weeknight dinner.

Caprese Avocado Salad with Balsamic Glaze

Ingredients:

- 2 large ripe avocados, sliced
- 2 cups cherry tomatoes, halved
- 1 1/2 cups fresh mozzarella balls (bocconcini)
- Fresh basil leaves, torn
- 2 tablespoons extra-virgin olive oil
- 2 tablespoons balsamic glaze
- Salt and black pepper, to taste

Instructions:

Prepare the Ingredients:
- Slice the avocados and halve the cherry tomatoes. If the mozzarella balls are large, you can cut them in half.

Assemble the Salad:
- Arrange the avocado slices, cherry tomatoes, and mozzarella balls on a serving platter or individual plates.

Add Fresh Basil:
- Scatter torn fresh basil leaves over the salad, distributing them evenly.

Drizzle with Olive Oil:
- Drizzle extra-virgin olive oil over the salad, ensuring all the ingredients are lightly coated.

Balsamic Glaze:
- Drizzle balsamic glaze over the salad. The sweet and tangy glaze adds a delightful finishing touch.

Season with Salt and Pepper:
- Season the Caprese Avocado Salad with salt and black pepper according to your taste preferences.

Serve Immediately:
- Serve the salad immediately, allowing the flavors to meld together. The creamy avocado, juicy tomatoes, and fresh mozzarella create a delicious combination.

This Caprese Avocado Salad is a refreshing and satisfying dish, perfect for a light lunch or as a side salad for dinner. The balsamic glaze adds a sweet and tangy element that enhances the overall flavor profile. Enjoy the vibrant colors and flavors of this delightful salad!

Mediterranean Chickpea Salad

Ingredients:

For the Salad:

- 2 cans (15 oz each) chickpeas, drained and rinsed
- 1 cucumber, diced
- 1 cup cherry tomatoes, halved
- 1 red bell pepper, diced
- 1/2 red onion, finely chopped
- 1/2 cup Kalamata olives, sliced
- 1/2 cup feta cheese, crumbled
- Fresh parsley, chopped, for garnish

For the Dressing:

- 1/4 cup extra-virgin olive oil
- 2 tablespoons red wine vinegar
- 1 clove garlic, minced
- 1 teaspoon dried oregano
- Salt and black pepper, to taste

Instructions:

Prepare the Chickpeas:
- Drain and rinse the chickpeas thoroughly. If you have time, you can pat them dry with a paper towel to remove excess moisture.

Assemble the Salad:
- In a large bowl, combine the chickpeas, diced cucumber, cherry tomatoes, red bell pepper, chopped red onion, Kalamata olives, and crumbled feta cheese.

Make the Dressing:
- In a small bowl, whisk together the extra-virgin olive oil, red wine vinegar, minced garlic, dried oregano, salt, and black pepper to create the dressing.

Dress the Salad:
- Pour the dressing over the salad and gently toss to coat all the ingredients evenly.

Chill and Marinate:
- Allow the Mediterranean Chickpea Salad to chill in the refrigerator for at least 30 minutes. This allows the flavors to meld together.

Garnish and Serve:
- Before serving, garnish the salad with chopped fresh parsley. Adjust seasoning if needed.

Serve and Enjoy:
- Serve the Mediterranean Chickpea Salad as a refreshing and nutritious side dish or as a light and satisfying meal on its own.

This salad is packed with protein, fiber, and the delightful flavors of the Mediterranean. It's perfect for picnics, potlucks, or as a quick and healthy lunch option. Enjoy the colorful and vibrant goodness of this Mediterranean-inspired dish!

Teriyaki Salmon with Broccoli

Ingredients:

For the Teriyaki Salmon:

- 4 salmon fillets
- 1/4 cup soy sauce
- 2 tablespoons mirin
- 2 tablespoons sake (or white wine)
- 2 tablespoons brown sugar
- 1 tablespoon honey
- 1 teaspoon grated ginger
- 1 teaspoon minced garlic
- 1 tablespoon vegetable oil
- Sesame seeds, for garnish (optional)
- Green onions, sliced, for garnish (optional)

For the Broccoli:

- 2 cups broccoli florets
- 1 tablespoon vegetable oil
- Salt and black pepper, to taste

For Serving:

- Cooked white or brown rice

Instructions:

Prepare the Teriyaki Marinade:
- In a bowl, whisk together soy sauce, mirin, sake, brown sugar, honey, grated ginger, and minced garlic to create the teriyaki marinade.

Marinate the Salmon:
- Place the salmon fillets in a shallow dish and pour half of the teriyaki marinade over them. Let them marinate for at least 15-30 minutes.

Cook the Salmon:
- Heat vegetable oil in a pan over medium-high heat. Remove the salmon from the marinade and cook for 3-4 minutes per side or until the salmon is cooked through and has a nice caramelized glaze. Baste the salmon with the remaining marinade as it cooks.

Prepare the Broccoli:
- In a separate pan, heat vegetable oil over medium heat. Add broccoli florets and sauté for 4-5 minutes or until the broccoli is tender-crisp. Season with salt and black pepper.

Serve:
- Serve the teriyaki salmon over cooked rice with sautéed broccoli on the side.

Garnish (Optional):
- Garnish the teriyaki salmon with sesame seeds and sliced green onions for added flavor and presentation.

Enjoy this Teriyaki Salmon with Broccoli for a flavorful and nutritious meal. The sweet and savory teriyaki glaze perfectly complements the tender salmon, and the broccoli adds a crisp and vibrant touch to the dish. Serve it over rice for a complete and satisfying meal.

Taco Stuffed Bell Peppers

Ingredients:

- 4 large bell peppers, halved and seeds removed
- 1 lb (450g) ground beef or turkey
- 1 small onion, diced
- 2 cloves garlic, minced
- 1 packet taco seasoning (or homemade seasoning)
- 1 can (15 oz) black beans, drained and rinsed
- 1 cup corn kernels (fresh, frozen, or canned)
- 1 cup diced tomatoes
- 1 cup shredded cheddar or Mexican blend cheese
- Fresh cilantro, chopped, for garnish (optional)
- Sour cream, for serving (optional)
- Salsa, for serving (optional)
- Avocado slices, for serving (optional)

Instructions:

Preheat the Oven:
- Preheat your oven to 375°F (190°C).

Prepare Bell Peppers:
- Cut the bell peppers in half lengthwise and remove the seeds and membranes. Place the pepper halves in a baking dish.

Cook Ground Meat:
- In a large skillet, cook the ground beef or turkey over medium heat until browned. Drain any excess fat.

Add Onion and Garlic:
- Add diced onion and minced garlic to the skillet with the cooked meat. Sauté for 2-3 minutes until the onion is softened.

Season with Taco Seasoning:
- Add the taco seasoning to the meat mixture, following the package instructions or your homemade seasoning recipe. Stir well to combine.

Add Black Beans, Corn, and Tomatoes:
- Mix in the black beans, corn, and diced tomatoes. Cook for an additional 2-3 minutes until heated through.

Stuff the Bell Peppers:
- Spoon the taco meat mixture into each bell pepper half, pressing down gently to pack the filling.

Bake:
- Sprinkle shredded cheese over the stuffed bell peppers. Bake in the preheated oven for about 20-25 minutes or until the peppers are tender.

Garnish and Serve:
- Remove from the oven and garnish with chopped cilantro if desired. Serve the taco stuffed bell peppers with optional toppings such as sour cream, salsa, and avocado slices.

Enjoy these Taco Stuffed Bell Peppers as a wholesome and flavorful alternative to traditional tacos. They are not only delicious but also a visually appealing way to serve a classic Mexican-inspired dish.

Pesto Chicken Quesadillas

Ingredients:

- 2 cups cooked chicken breast, shredded
- 1/2 cup pesto sauce (store-bought or homemade)
- 4 large flour tortillas
- 2 cups shredded mozzarella cheese
- 1 cup cherry tomatoes, sliced
- 1/4 cup fresh basil, chopped
- Olive oil, for cooking
- Salt and black pepper, to taste
- Sour cream and salsa, for serving (optional)

Instructions:

Prepare the Chicken:
- Shred the cooked chicken breast into bite-sized pieces. Season with salt and black pepper to taste.

Mix Chicken with Pesto:
- In a bowl, combine the shredded chicken with pesto sauce. Mix well to coat the chicken evenly with the pesto.

Assemble the Quesadillas:
- Place one tortilla on a clean surface. Spread a portion of the pesto chicken mixture over half of the tortilla. Add a layer of shredded mozzarella, sliced cherry tomatoes, and chopped fresh basil. Fold the tortilla in half, creating a quesadilla.

Cook the Quesadillas:
- Heat a pan or griddle over medium heat. Drizzle with olive oil. Place the assembled quesadilla in the pan and cook for 2-3 minutes on each side or until the tortilla is golden brown, and the cheese is melted. Repeat for the remaining quesadillas.

Slice and Serve:
- Remove the quesadillas from the pan and let them cool for a minute. Slice each quesadilla into wedges.

Serve with Toppings:
- Serve the Pesto Chicken Quesadillas with optional toppings like sour cream and salsa.

Enjoy these Pesto Chicken Quesadillas as a quick and tasty meal. The combination of pesto, chicken, and melted cheese creates a delightful flavor that's perfect for a simple lunch or dinner.

Sesame Ginger Beef and Vegetable Stir-Fry

Ingredients:

For the Stir-Fry Sauce:

- 1/4 cup soy sauce
- 2 tablespoons hoisin sauce
- 1 tablespoon rice vinegar
- 1 tablespoon sesame oil
- 1 tablespoon honey
- 1 tablespoon grated ginger
- 2 cloves garlic, minced
- 1 teaspoon cornstarch

For the Stir-Fry:

- 1 lb (450g) beef sirloin or flank steak, thinly sliced
- 2 tablespoons vegetable oil, divided
- 1 bell pepper, thinly sliced
- 1 cup broccoli florets
- 1 carrot, julienned
- 1 cup snap peas, ends trimmed
- 2 green onions, sliced
- Sesame seeds, for garnish (optional)
- Cooked rice or noodles, for serving

Instructions:

Prepare the Stir-Fry Sauce:
- In a bowl, whisk together soy sauce, hoisin sauce, rice vinegar, sesame oil, honey, grated ginger, minced garlic, and cornstarch. Set aside.

Slice and Marinate the Beef:
- Thinly slice the beef and place it in a bowl. Pour half of the prepared stir-fry sauce over the beef, toss to coat, and let it marinate for about 15-30 minutes.

Heat the Pan:
- Heat 1 tablespoon of vegetable oil in a wok or large skillet over high heat.

Stir-Fry the Beef:

- Add the marinated beef to the hot pan and stir-fry for 2-3 minutes or until the beef is browned and cooked through. Remove the beef from the pan and set aside.

Stir-Fry Vegetables:
- In the same pan, add the remaining 1 tablespoon of vegetable oil. Add bell pepper, broccoli, carrot, and snap peas. Stir-fry for 3-4 minutes or until the vegetables are crisp-tender.

Combine and Finish:
- Add the cooked beef back to the pan with the vegetables. Pour the remaining stir-fry sauce over the mixture. Toss everything together until well-coated and heated through.

Garnish and Serve:
- Garnish with sliced green onions and sesame seeds if desired. Serve the Sesame Ginger Beef and Vegetable Stir-Fry over cooked rice or noodles.

Enjoy this flavorful and nutritious stir-fry that's perfect for a quick and satisfying dinner. The combination of sesame and ginger adds a delightful depth of flavor to the beef and vegetables.

One-Pan Lemon Herb Chicken with Veggies

Ingredients:

- 4 boneless, skinless chicken breasts
- 1 lb (450g) baby potatoes, halved
- 1 cup baby carrots
- 1 cup cherry tomatoes
- 1 zucchini, sliced
- 1/4 cup olive oil
- 3 tablespoons fresh lemon juice
- 3 cloves garlic, minced
- 1 teaspoon dried oregano
- 1 teaspoon dried thyme
- Salt and black pepper, to taste
- Fresh parsley, chopped, for garnish

Instructions:

Preheat the Oven:
- Preheat your oven to 400°F (200°C).

Prepare the Chicken and Veggies:
- Place the chicken breasts, halved baby potatoes, baby carrots, cherry tomatoes, and sliced zucchini on a large baking sheet.

Make the Lemon Herb Marinade:
- In a small bowl, whisk together olive oil, fresh lemon juice, minced garlic, dried oregano, dried thyme, salt, and black pepper.

Coat Chicken and Veggies:
- Pour the lemon herb marinade over the chicken and veggies. Toss everything to coat evenly.

Arrange on Baking Sheet:
- Arrange the chicken and veggies in a single layer on the baking sheet, ensuring they are well-spaced.

Bake in the Oven:
- Bake in the preheated oven for about 25-30 minutes or until the chicken is cooked through and the veggies are tender. You can check the chicken's internal temperature, which should reach 165°F (74°C).

Garnish and Serve:
- Remove from the oven, garnish with chopped fresh parsley, and serve the One-Pan Lemon Herb Chicken with Veggies immediately.

This one-pan meal is not only delicious but also convenient for busy days. The lemon and herbs infuse the chicken and veggies with bright flavors, and the one-pan cooking method makes cleanup a breeze. Enjoy this wholesome and flavorful dish!

Shrimp and Asparagus Stir-Fry

Ingredients:

- 1 lb (450g) large shrimp, peeled and deveined
- 1 bunch asparagus, trimmed and cut into bite-sized pieces
- 3 tablespoons soy sauce
- 2 tablespoons oyster sauce
- 1 tablespoon hoisin sauce
- 1 tablespoon rice vinegar
- 1 tablespoon sesame oil
- 2 tablespoons vegetable oil
- 3 cloves garlic, minced
- 1 teaspoon grated ginger
- Red pepper flakes, to taste (optional)
- Sesame seeds, for garnish (optional)
- Cooked rice, for serving

Instructions:

Prepare Shrimp and Asparagus:
- Pat the shrimp dry with paper towels. In a bowl, mix the soy sauce, oyster sauce, hoisin sauce, and rice vinegar to create the sauce. Set aside.

Stir-Fry Shrimp:
- Heat 1 tablespoon of vegetable oil in a wok or large skillet over medium-high heat. Add the shrimp and stir-fry for 2-3 minutes or until they turn pink and opaque. Remove the shrimp from the pan and set aside.

Stir-Fry Asparagus:
- In the same pan, add another tablespoon of vegetable oil. Stir in the minced garlic and grated ginger. Add the asparagus and stir-fry for 3-4 minutes until they are tender-crisp.

Combine Shrimp and Asparagus:
- Return the cooked shrimp to the pan with the asparagus. Pour the prepared sauce over the shrimp and asparagus. Toss everything together until well-coated and heated through.

Finish the Dish:
- Drizzle sesame oil over the stir-fry and toss to combine. If desired, add red pepper flakes for a bit of heat.

Garnish and Serve:

- Garnish the Shrimp and Asparagus Stir-Fry with sesame seeds if desired. Serve over cooked rice.

This quick and tasty stir-fry is perfect for a busy weeknight dinner. The combination of succulent shrimp and crisp asparagus, coated in a flavorful sauce, makes for a delicious and well-balanced meal. Enjoy over a bed of rice for a satisfying and wholesome dish.

Cajun Chicken Pasta

Ingredients:

- 8 oz (225g) fettuccine pasta
- 2 boneless, skinless chicken breasts, thinly sliced
- Cajun seasoning (store-bought or homemade)
- 2 tablespoons olive oil
- 1 red bell pepper, thinly sliced
- 1 green bell pepper, thinly sliced
- 1 small red onion, thinly sliced
- 3 cloves garlic, minced
- 1 cup cherry tomatoes, halved
- 1 cup heavy cream
- 1/2 cup chicken broth
- 1 teaspoon paprika
- 1/2 teaspoon dried thyme
- Salt and black pepper, to taste
- Fresh parsley, chopped, for garnish

Instructions:

Cook the Pasta:
- Cook the fettuccine pasta according to the package instructions. Drain and set aside.

Season the Chicken:
- Season the sliced chicken breasts with Cajun seasoning, ensuring they are well coated.

Cook Chicken:
- In a large skillet, heat olive oil over medium-high heat. Add the seasoned chicken and cook for 3-4 minutes per side or until cooked through and nicely browned. Remove the chicken from the skillet and set aside.

Sauté Vegetables:
- In the same skillet, add a bit more olive oil if needed. Sauté the sliced red and green bell peppers, red onion, and minced garlic until the vegetables are tender.

Prepare Cajun Cream Sauce:
- Pour in the heavy cream and chicken broth, stirring to combine. Add paprika, dried thyme, salt, and black pepper. Let the sauce simmer for a few minutes to thicken.

Combine Pasta and Chicken:
- Add the cooked fettuccine pasta and sliced Cajun-seasoned chicken back to the skillet. Toss everything together until the pasta and chicken are well coated with the creamy Cajun sauce.

Add Cherry Tomatoes:
- Add the halved cherry tomatoes and toss briefly until they are heated through.

Garnish and Serve:
- Garnish the Cajun Chicken Pasta with chopped fresh parsley. Serve immediately.

Enjoy this spicy and creamy Cajun Chicken Pasta as a flavorful and satisfying dinner. The combination of the Cajun-seasoned chicken, colorful vegetables, and creamy sauce creates a delicious and comforting meal.

Caprese Chicken Skillet

Ingredients:

- 4 boneless, skinless chicken breasts
- Salt and black pepper, to taste
- 1 tablespoon olive oil
- 2 cloves garlic, minced
- 1 cup cherry tomatoes, halved
- 8 oz (225g) fresh mozzarella, sliced
- Balsamic glaze, for drizzling
- Fresh basil leaves, for garnish

Instructions:

Season and Cook Chicken:
- Season the chicken breasts with salt and black pepper on both sides. In a large skillet, heat olive oil over medium-high heat. Add the chicken breasts and cook for 5-6 minutes per side or until they reach an internal temperature of 165°F (74°C). Remove the chicken from the skillet and set aside.

Sauté Garlic and Tomatoes:
- In the same skillet, add minced garlic and sauté for about 1 minute. Add the halved cherry tomatoes and cook for an additional 2-3 minutes until they start to soften.

Return Chicken to Skillet:
- Return the cooked chicken breasts to the skillet, nestling them among the tomatoes.

Top with Mozzarella:
- Place slices of fresh mozzarella on top of each chicken breast. Cover the skillet with a lid and let it cook for an additional 2-3 minutes until the cheese is melted and bubbly.

Drizzle with Balsamic Glaze:
- Drizzle balsamic glaze over the chicken and tomatoes. You can adjust the amount to your liking.

Garnish and Serve:
- Garnish the Caprese Chicken Skillet with fresh basil leaves. Serve the chicken directly from the skillet or transfer to a serving platter.

This Caprese Chicken Skillet is a delicious and elegant dish that's perfect for a quick and flavorful dinner. The combination of juicy chicken, sweet cherry tomatoes, and creamy mozzarella, topped with a balsamic glaze, creates a delightful meal with the essence of a Caprese salad.

Vegetarian Black Bean and Corn Quesadillas

Ingredients:

- 1 can (15 oz) black beans, drained and rinsed
- 1 cup corn kernels (fresh, frozen, or canned)
- 1 cup diced bell peppers (any color)
- 1/2 cup diced red onion
- 1 teaspoon ground cumin
- 1 teaspoon chili powder
- Salt and black pepper, to taste
- 4 large flour tortillas
- 2 cups shredded Mexican cheese blend
- Cooking spray or vegetable oil, for cooking
- Salsa, guacamole, or sour cream, for serving (optional)

Instructions:

Prepare the Filling:
- In a bowl, combine the black beans, corn, diced bell peppers, diced red onion, ground cumin, chili powder, salt, and black pepper. Mix well to combine.

Assemble the Quesadillas:
- Place a tortilla on a flat surface. Spoon a portion of the black bean and corn filling onto one half of the tortilla. Sprinkle a generous amount of shredded cheese over the filling. Fold the tortilla in half to create a quesadilla.

Cook the Quesadillas:
- Heat a large skillet or griddle over medium heat. Lightly coat the surface with cooking spray or a small amount of vegetable oil. Place the assembled quesadilla in the skillet and cook for 2-3 minutes on each side or until the tortilla is golden brown and the cheese is melted.

Repeat:
- Repeat the process with the remaining tortillas and filling.

Slice and Serve:
- Once cooked, remove the quesadillas from the skillet and let them cool for a moment. Slice each quesadilla into wedges.

Serve with Optional Toppings:
- Serve the Vegetarian Black Bean and Corn Quesadillas with salsa, guacamole, or sour cream if desired.

These quesadillas are not only easy to make but also packed with flavor and a satisfying combination of textures. They make for a great meatless meal option that's perfect for lunch or dinner. Enjoy the delicious blend of black beans, corn, and melted cheese in every bite!

Honey Garlic Glazed Salmon

Ingredients:

- 4 salmon fillets
- Salt and black pepper, to taste
- 3 tablespoons honey
- 2 tablespoons soy sauce
- 1 tablespoon Dijon mustard
- 2 cloves garlic, minced
- 1 tablespoon olive oil
- Sesame seeds and chopped green onions, for garnish (optional)

Instructions:

Preheat the Oven:
- Preheat your oven to 400°F (200°C).

Season Salmon:
- Season the salmon fillets with salt and black pepper.

Make the Honey Garlic Glaze:
- In a small bowl, whisk together honey, soy sauce, Dijon mustard, and minced garlic to create the glaze.

Sear Salmon:
- Heat olive oil in an oven-safe skillet over medium-high heat. Sear the salmon fillets, skin-side up, for 2-3 minutes until they get a golden crust.

Brush with Glaze:
- Brush the tops of the salmon fillets with the honey garlic glaze.

Bake in the Oven:
- Transfer the skillet to the preheated oven and bake for 8-10 minutes or until the salmon is cooked through. The internal temperature should reach 145°F (63°C).

Glaze Again:
- During the last few minutes of baking, brush the salmon with additional glaze.

Garnish and Serve:
- Remove the salmon from the oven, and if desired, garnish with sesame seeds and chopped green onions. Serve the Honey Garlic Glazed Salmon over rice or your favorite side.

This Honey Garlic Glazed Salmon is a perfect combination of sweet and savory flavors, making it a crowd-pleaser. The glaze adds a beautiful shine and enhances the natural richness of the salmon. Enjoy this simple and flavorful dish for a quick and satisfying meal.

Mushroom and Spinach Risotto

Ingredients:

- 1 cup Arborio rice
- 1/2 cup dry white wine (optional)
- 4 cups vegetable or chicken broth, kept warm
- 2 tablespoons olive oil
- 1 small onion, finely chopped
- 2 cloves garlic, minced
- 8 oz (225g) mushrooms, sliced (button, cremini, or shiitake)
- 2 cups fresh spinach, chopped
- 1/2 cup Parmesan cheese, grated
- Salt and black pepper, to taste
- Fresh parsley, chopped, for garnish

Instructions:

    Prepare the Broth:
- Heat the vegetable or chicken broth in a saucepan and keep it warm over low heat.

    Sauté Onion and Garlic:
- In a large skillet or wide saucepan, heat olive oil over medium heat. Add the finely chopped onion and sauté until it becomes translucent.

    Cook Mushrooms:
- Add the minced garlic and sliced mushrooms to the skillet. Cook for 5-7 minutes until the mushrooms are tender and have released their moisture.

    Toast the Rice:
- Add Arborio rice to the skillet and cook for 1-2 minutes, stirring frequently, until the rice is lightly toasted.

    Deglaze with Wine (Optional):
- Pour in the white wine (if using) and stir until it is mostly absorbed by the rice.

    Add Broth:
- Begin adding the warm broth to the rice one ladle at a time, stirring constantly. Allow the liquid to be absorbed before adding the next ladle. Continue this process until the rice is creamy and cooked to al dente, which usually takes about 18-20 minutes.

    Add Spinach:

- In the last 5 minutes of cooking, add the chopped fresh spinach to the risotto and stir until wilted.

Finish and Season:
- Once the rice is cooked, stir in the grated Parmesan cheese. Season with salt and black pepper to taste.

Garnish and Serve:
- Garnish the Mushroom and Spinach Risotto with fresh chopped parsley. Serve immediately.

Enjoy this creamy and flavorful Mushroom and Spinach Risotto as a comforting and elegant meal. The combination of mushrooms, spinach, and Parmesan creates a rich and satisfying dish that's perfect for a special dinner or a cozy night at home.

Buffalo Chicken Lettuce Wraps

Ingredients:

For the Buffalo Chicken:

- 2 cups cooked and shredded chicken (rotisserie chicken works well)
- 1/2 cup buffalo sauce
- 2 tablespoons melted butter
- 1 tablespoon ranch dressing
- 1 teaspoon garlic powder
- Salt and black pepper, to taste

For Assembling Lettuce Wraps:

- Large lettuce leaves (such as iceberg or butter lettuce)
- Celery sticks, sliced
- Carrot sticks, sliced
- Ranch or blue cheese dressing, for drizzling
- Fresh parsley or cilantro, chopped, for garnish

Instructions:

    Prepare the Buffalo Chicken:
- In a bowl, combine the shredded chicken with buffalo sauce, melted butter, ranch dressing, garlic powder, salt, and black pepper. Mix until the chicken is well-coated.

    Assemble Lettuce Wraps:
- Take large lettuce leaves and spoon the buffalo chicken mixture onto each leaf.

    Add Toppings:
- Top the buffalo chicken with sliced celery and carrot sticks.

    Drizzle with Dressing:
- Drizzle ranch or blue cheese dressing over the top of each lettuce wrap.

    Garnish:
- Garnish the Buffalo Chicken Lettuce Wraps with fresh chopped parsley or cilantro.

    Serve:
- Serve the lettuce wraps immediately. Enjoy them as a light and flavorful meal or snack.

These Buffalo Chicken Lettuce Wraps offer a satisfying combination of spicy buffalo chicken with crisp lettuce and crunchy vegetables. They are perfect for a quick lunch, dinner, or as an appetizer for parties. Customize the toppings to your liking and enjoy a low-carb twist on classic buffalo chicken flavors.

Easy Beef and Broccoli

Ingredients:

For the Beef Marinade:

- 1 lb (450g) flank steak, thinly sliced
- 2 tablespoons soy sauce
- 1 tablespoon oyster sauce
- 1 tablespoon cornstarch
- 1 teaspoon sesame oil
- 1 teaspoon sugar
- 1/2 teaspoon black pepper

For the Stir-Fry:

- 2 tablespoons vegetable oil, divided
- 3 cups broccoli florets
- 2 cloves garlic, minced
- 1 teaspoon ginger, grated
- 1/4 cup soy sauce
- 2 tablespoons oyster sauce
- 1 tablespoon hoisin sauce
- 1 tablespoon cornstarch (mixed with 2 tablespoons water to make a slurry)
- Cooked rice, for serving
- Sesame seeds and green onions, for garnish (optional)

Instructions:

Marinate the Beef:
- In a bowl, combine the sliced flank steak with soy sauce, oyster sauce, cornstarch, sesame oil, sugar, and black pepper. Let it marinate for at least 15-30 minutes.

Stir-Fry the Broccoli:
- Heat 1 tablespoon of vegetable oil in a wok or large skillet over medium-high heat. Add the broccoli florets and stir-fry for 3-4 minutes until they are crisp-tender. Remove the broccoli from the pan and set aside.

Cook the Beef:

- In the same pan, add another tablespoon of vegetable oil. Add the marinated beef, minced garlic, and grated ginger. Stir-fry for 2-3 minutes until the beef is browned and cooked through.

Combine Beef and Broccoli:
- Return the cooked broccoli to the pan with the beef. Stir to combine.

Prepare the Sauce:
- In a small bowl, mix soy sauce, oyster sauce, hoisin sauce, and the cornstarch slurry.

Add the Sauce:
- Pour the sauce mixture over the beef and broccoli. Stir continuously until the sauce thickens and coats the beef and broccoli.

Serve:
- Serve the Easy Beef and Broccoli over cooked rice. Garnish with sesame seeds and chopped green onions if desired.

This Easy Beef and Broccoli recipe provides a flavorful and satisfying meal with tender beef and crisp broccoli. It's a perfect dish for a quick weeknight dinner, and you can customize it by adding your favorite vegetables or adjusting the level of spiciness. Enjoy!

Lemon Butter Garlic Shrimp

Ingredients:

- 1 lb (450g) large shrimp, peeled and deveined
- Salt and black pepper, to taste
- 2 tablespoons olive oil
- 4 cloves garlic, minced
- 1/2 cup chicken broth or white wine
- Juice of 1 lemon
- Zest of 1 lemon
- 2 tablespoons unsalted butter
- 2 tablespoons fresh parsley, chopped
- Red pepper flakes (optional, for a bit of heat)
- Cooked pasta or rice, for serving

Instructions:

Prepare Shrimp:
- Pat the shrimp dry with paper towels and season with salt and black pepper.

Sear Shrimp:
- In a large skillet, heat olive oil over medium-high heat. Add the shrimp to the skillet and cook for 1-2 minutes per side or until they turn pink and opaque. Remove the shrimp from the skillet and set aside.

Sauté Garlic:
- In the same skillet, add minced garlic and sauté for about 30 seconds until fragrant.

Deglaze with Broth or Wine:
- Pour in the chicken broth or white wine, scraping the bottom of the skillet to release any browned bits. Allow it to simmer for 2-3 minutes to reduce slightly.

Add Lemon Juice and Zest:
- Add the lemon juice and zest to the skillet, stirring to combine.

Finish with Butter:
- Reduce the heat to low and add the unsalted butter to the skillet. Swirl the butter into the sauce until melted and well combined.

Return Shrimp:

- Return the cooked shrimp to the skillet and toss them in the lemon butter garlic sauce. Cook for an additional 1-2 minutes to heat the shrimp through.

Season and Garnish:
- Season the dish with additional salt and black pepper if needed. If desired, add red pepper flakes for a bit of heat. Sprinkle fresh chopped parsley over the shrimp.

Serve:
- Serve the Lemon Butter Garlic Shrimp over cooked pasta or rice.

Enjoy this Lemon Butter Garlic Shrimp dish for a quick and elegant meal. The combination of citrusy lemon, garlic, and butter creates a flavorful sauce that complements the succulent shrimp. Serve it over your favorite pasta or rice for a delightful and satisfying dinner.

Margherita Flatbread Pizza

Ingredients:

- 1 large flatbread or pre-made pizza crust
- 1 tablespoon olive oil
- 2 cloves garlic, minced
- 1 cup cherry tomatoes, halved
- 8 oz (225g) fresh mozzarella, sliced
- Fresh basil leaves
- Salt and black pepper, to taste
- Balsamic glaze, for drizzling (optional)

Instructions:

Preheat the Oven:
- Preheat your oven according to the flatbread or pizza crust package instructions.

Prepare the Flatbread:
- Place the flatbread or pizza crust on a baking sheet.

Brush with Olive Oil:
- In a small bowl, mix the minced garlic with olive oil. Brush the olive oil mixture over the flatbread, ensuring even coverage.

Assemble the Pizza:
- Arrange the sliced fresh mozzarella over the flatbread. Scatter the halved cherry tomatoes on top. Season with salt and black pepper to taste.

Bake in the Oven:
- Bake the pizza in the preheated oven according to the flatbread or pizza crust package instructions, or until the cheese is melted and bubbly.

Add Fresh Basil:
- Once out of the oven, scatter fresh basil leaves over the hot pizza.

Drizzle with Balsamic Glaze (Optional):
- If desired, drizzle balsamic glaze over the Margherita Flatbread Pizza for added sweetness and flavor.

Slice and Serve:
- Slice the pizza into portions and serve immediately.

This Margherita Flatbread Pizza is a quick and delicious option for a light meal or appetizer. The combination of fresh tomatoes, creamy mozzarella, and aromatic basil creates a classic and timeless flavor. Enjoy the simplicity and elegance of this Margherita pizza!

Chicken Piccata with Lemon Caper Sauce

Ingredients:

For the Chicken:

- 4 boneless, skinless chicken breasts
- Salt and black pepper, to taste
- 1 cup all-purpose flour, for dredging
- 2 tablespoons olive oil
- 4 tablespoons unsalted butter

For the Lemon Caper Sauce:

- 1/2 cup chicken broth
- Juice of 2 lemons
- 1/4 cup capers, drained
- 1/4 cup fresh parsley, chopped
- Salt and black pepper, to taste

Instructions:

Prepare the Chicken:
- Season the chicken breasts with salt and black pepper. Dredge each chicken breast in flour, shaking off any excess.

Pan-Sear the Chicken:
- In a large skillet, heat olive oil and 2 tablespoons of butter over medium-high heat. Add the chicken breasts to the skillet and cook for about 4-5 minutes per side or until golden brown and cooked through. Remove the chicken from the skillet and set aside.

Make the Lemon Caper Sauce:
- In the same skillet, add chicken broth, lemon juice, capers, and chopped parsley. Bring the mixture to a simmer, scraping up any browned bits from the bottom of the skillet.

Adjust Seasoning:
- Season the sauce with salt and black pepper to taste. Adjust the thickness of the sauce by simmering for an additional minute if needed.

Finish the Dish:

- Add the remaining 2 tablespoons of butter to the sauce and swirl until melted. Return the cooked chicken breasts to the skillet, spooning the sauce over them. Allow the chicken to heat through for a minute or two.

Serve:
- Plate the Chicken Piccata and Lemon Caper Sauce. Garnish with additional chopped parsley if desired.

Optional: Pasta or Rice:
- Serve the Chicken Piccata with your choice of pasta or rice to soak up the delicious lemon caper sauce.

This Chicken Piccata with Lemon Caper Sauce is a delightful and elegant dish that's perfect for a special dinner. The combination of the tangy lemon, briny capers, and savory chicken creates a mouthwatering flavor profile. Enjoy the richness of the sauce paired with the tender and crispy chicken.

Zucchini Noodles with Pesto and Cherry Tomatoes

Ingredients:

- 4 medium zucchini, spiralized into noodles
- 1 cup cherry tomatoes, halved
- 1/2 cup homemade or store-bought pesto
- 2 tablespoons pine nuts, toasted (optional)
- Grated Parmesan cheese, for serving
- Salt and black pepper, to taste
- Fresh basil leaves, for garnish

Instructions:

Spiralize Zucchini:
- Use a spiralizer to turn the zucchini into noodles. If you don't have a spiralizer, you can use a julienne peeler or a vegetable peeler to create thin strips.

Prepare Pesto:
- If you don't have store-bought pesto, you can make your own by blending fresh basil, garlic, pine nuts, Parmesan cheese, and olive oil in a food processor. Adjust the ingredients to taste.

Cook Zucchini Noodles:
- In a large skillet over medium heat, add a small amount of olive oil. Add the zucchini noodles and cook for 2-3 minutes, tossing gently until they are just heated through. Be careful not to overcook, as zucchini noodles can become mushy.

Combine with Pesto and Tomatoes:
- Add the halved cherry tomatoes to the skillet with the zucchini noodles. Stir in the pesto and toss until everything is well combined and heated through.

Season and Toast Pine Nuts:
- Season the dish with salt and black pepper to taste. If using, toast the pine nuts in a dry pan over medium heat until golden brown, then sprinkle them over the zucchini noodles.

Serve:
- Divide the Zucchini Noodles with Pesto and Cherry Tomatoes among plates. Garnish with grated Parmesan cheese and fresh basil leaves.

This dish is not only healthy and vibrant but also quick to prepare. The combination of zucchini noodles, pesto, and sweet cherry tomatoes creates a refreshing and satisfying meal. Customize it by adding grilled chicken, shrimp, or your favorite protein if desired. Enjoy this light and delicious zoodle dish!

Quick and Healthy Turkey Chili

Ingredients:

- 1 lb (450g) ground turkey
- 1 tablespoon olive oil
- 1 onion, diced
- 3 cloves garlic, minced
- 1 bell pepper, diced (any color)
- 1 zucchini, diced
- 1 can (15 oz) kidney beans, drained and rinsed
- 1 can (15 oz) black beans, drained and rinsed
- 1 can (15 oz) diced tomatoes
- 1 cup corn kernels (fresh, frozen, or canned)
- 1 cup low-sodium chicken broth
- 2 tablespoons chili powder
- 1 teaspoon cumin
- 1 teaspoon paprika
- 1/2 teaspoon oregano
- Salt and black pepper, to taste
- Optional toppings: shredded cheese, sliced green onions, Greek yogurt or sour cream, chopped cilantro

Instructions:

Cook Ground Turkey:
- In a large pot or Dutch oven, heat olive oil over medium heat. Add ground turkey and cook until browned, breaking it apart with a spoon as it cooks.

Sauté Vegetables:
- Add diced onion, minced garlic, bell pepper, and zucchini to the pot. Sauté for 5-7 minutes until the vegetables are softened.

Add Beans and Tomatoes:
- Stir in kidney beans, black beans, diced tomatoes (with their juices), and corn.

Season and Simmer:
- Add chili powder, cumin, paprika, oregano, salt, and black pepper. Pour in the chicken broth and stir to combine. Bring the chili to a simmer, then reduce the heat to low, cover, and let it simmer for at least 15-20 minutes to allow the flavors to meld.

Adjust Seasoning:

- Taste and adjust the seasoning if needed. Add more chili powder, cumin, or salt according to your preference.

Serve:
- Ladle the Quick and Healthy Turkey Chili into bowls. Top with your favorite toppings such as shredded cheese, sliced green onions, Greek yogurt or sour cream, and chopped cilantro.

This turkey chili is not only quick and easy to make but also a healthier alternative to traditional beef chili. Packed with protein and colorful vegetables, it's a satisfying and comforting meal. Enjoy it on its own or with your favorite toppings!

Garlic Parmesan Crusted Tilapia

Ingredients:

- 4 tilapia fillets
- 1/2 cup grated Parmesan cheese
- 1/4 cup breadcrumbs
- 2 cloves garlic, minced
- 1 teaspoon dried oregano
- 1 teaspoon dried parsley
- 1/2 teaspoon paprika
- Salt and black pepper, to taste
- 2 tablespoons olive oil
- Lemon wedges, for serving

Instructions:

Preheat the Oven:
- Preheat your oven to 400°F (200°C). Line a baking sheet with parchment paper or lightly grease it.

Prepare the Coating:
- In a shallow dish, combine the grated Parmesan cheese, breadcrumbs, minced garlic, dried oregano, dried parsley, paprika, salt, and black pepper. Mix well.

Coat the Tilapia:
- Pat the tilapia fillets dry with a paper towel. Dip each fillet into the Parmesan mixture, pressing the coating onto both sides of the fish to adhere.

Pan-Sear:
- In an oven-safe skillet, heat olive oil over medium-high heat. Once the oil is hot, add the tilapia fillets and sear for 2-3 minutes on each side or until the crust is golden brown.

Finish in the Oven:
- Transfer the skillet to the preheated oven and bake for an additional 8-10 minutes, or until the tilapia is cooked through and flakes easily with a fork.

Serve:
- Remove the Garlic Parmesan Crusted Tilapia from the oven. Serve the fillets with lemon wedges for squeezing over the top.

This Garlic Parmesan Crusted Tilapia is a tasty and satisfying dish that's quick to prepare. The combination of garlic, Parmesan, and herbs creates a flavorful crust that adds depth to the mild tilapia. Serve it with your favorite side dishes for a delightful and wholesome meal.

Thai Basil Chicken Stir-Fry

Ingredients:

- 1 lb (450g) boneless, skinless chicken thighs or breasts, finely chopped or ground
- 2 tablespoons vegetable oil
- 4 cloves garlic, minced
- 2 Thai bird chilies, finely chopped (adjust to your spice preference)
- 1 cup fresh basil leaves, loosely packed
- 1 bell pepper, thinly sliced
- 1 onion, thinly sliced
- 2 tablespoons oyster sauce
- 1 tablespoon soy sauce
- 1 teaspoon fish sauce
- 1 teaspoon sugar
- 1/2 cup chicken broth
- Cooked jasmine rice, for serving
- Fried egg, for serving (optional)

Instructions:

Prepare Ingredients:
- Finely chop or ground the chicken. Mince the garlic, chop the Thai bird chilies, slice the bell pepper and onion, and set aside the fresh basil leaves.

Make Sauce:
- In a small bowl, mix together oyster sauce, soy sauce, fish sauce, and sugar. Set aside.

Stir-Fry Chicken:
- Heat vegetable oil in a wok or large skillet over high heat. Add minced garlic and chopped Thai bird chilies. Stir-fry for 30 seconds until fragrant.

Cook Chicken:
- Add the finely chopped or ground chicken to the wok. Cook, breaking it apart with a spatula, until the chicken is cooked through and no longer pink.

Add Vegetables:
- Add sliced bell pepper and onion to the wok. Stir-fry for an additional 2-3 minutes until the vegetables are slightly softened.

Add Sauce:

- Pour the prepared sauce over the chicken and vegetables. Stir to coat evenly.

Add Basil Leaves:
- Add fresh basil leaves to the wok and stir-fry for 1-2 minutes until the basil is wilted.

Adjust Seasoning:
- Taste the stir-fry and adjust the seasoning if needed. You can add more soy sauce, fish sauce, or sugar according to your taste preferences.

Finish and Serve:
- Pour chicken broth over the stir-fry to create a bit of sauciness. Stir well and cook for an additional minute.

Serve:
- Serve the Thai Basil Chicken Stir-Fry over cooked jasmine rice. Optionally, top with a fried egg for an extra touch.

Enjoy this Thai Basil Chicken Stir-Fry for a quick and flavorful meal that captures the essence of Thai cuisine! Adjust the level of spiciness to suit your taste, and feel free to customize the vegetables to your liking.

Mango Salsa Chicken Bowls

Ingredients:

For the Grilled Chicken:

- 1.5 lbs (680g) boneless, skinless chicken breasts
- 2 tablespoons olive oil
- 1 teaspoon ground cumin
- 1 teaspoon chili powder
- Salt and black pepper, to taste

For the Mango Salsa:

- 2 ripe mangoes, peeled, pitted, and diced
- 1/2 red onion, finely chopped
- 1 red bell pepper, diced
- 1 jalapeño, seeded and finely chopped
- 1/4 cup fresh cilantro, chopped
- Juice of 2 limes
- Salt, to taste

For Serving:

- Cooked quinoa or rice
- Avocado slices (optional)
- Lime wedges for garnish

Instructions:

Preheat Grill:
- Preheat your grill to medium-high heat.

Season Chicken:
- In a bowl, mix olive oil, ground cumin, chili powder, salt, and black pepper. Brush the chicken breasts with this mixture.

Grill Chicken:
- Grill the chicken breasts for 6-8 minutes per side or until fully cooked and juices run clear. Cooking times may vary depending on the thickness of the chicken.

Rest and Slice:

- Remove the chicken from the grill and let it rest for a few minutes. Slice it into thin strips.

Prepare Mango Salsa:
- In a separate bowl, combine diced mangoes, chopped red onion, diced red bell pepper, jalapeño, cilantro, lime juice, and a pinch of salt. Mix well.

Assemble Bowls:
- In serving bowls, layer cooked quinoa or rice. Top with sliced grilled chicken and generous spoonfuls of mango salsa.

Garnish:
- Garnish the bowls with avocado slices (if using) and lime wedges.

Serve:
- Serve the Mango Salsa Chicken Bowls immediately, allowing everyone to squeeze lime over their bowls for extra flavor.

This dish is a delightful combination of grilled chicken's savory goodness and the sweet, tangy freshness of mango salsa. It's a perfect option for a healthy and flavorful meal. Enjoy the vibrant colors and delicious flavors of these Mango Salsa Chicken Bowls!

Mushroom and Spinach Quesadillas

Ingredients:

- 8 small flour tortillas
- 2 cups fresh spinach, chopped
- 2 cups mushrooms, sliced
- 1 small onion, finely chopped
- 2 cloves garlic, minced
- 1 cup shredded Monterey Jack or mozzarella cheese
- 1 cup shredded cheddar cheese
- 2 tablespoons olive oil
- Salt and black pepper, to taste
- Optional toppings: salsa, guacamole, sour cream

Instructions:

Sauté Vegetables:
- In a large skillet, heat olive oil over medium heat. Add chopped onions and minced garlic, sautéing until softened.

Add Mushrooms:
- Add sliced mushrooms to the skillet and cook until they release their moisture and become golden brown.

Add Spinach:
- Add chopped spinach to the skillet and cook until wilted. Season with salt and black pepper to taste. Remove from heat.

Assemble Quesadillas:
- Place a tortilla on a flat surface. Spread a portion of the mushroom and spinach mixture over half of the tortilla. Sprinkle a mix of Monterey Jack or mozzarella cheese and cheddar cheese over the veggies.

Fold and Cook:
- Fold the tortilla in half, pressing gently. Repeat with the remaining tortillas.

Cook on Griddle or Skillet:
- Heat a griddle or large skillet over medium heat. Cook the quesadillas for about 2-3 minutes on each side or until the tortillas are golden brown and the cheese is melted.

Slice and Serve:
- Remove from the heat and let them cool for a moment. Slice each quesadilla into wedges.

Serve with Toppings:

- Serve Mushroom and Spinach Quesadillas with your favorite toppings such as salsa, guacamole, and sour cream.

These Mushroom and Spinach Quesadillas are a great vegetarian option for a quick lunch or dinner. The combination of sautéed mushrooms, spinach, and melted cheese creates a savory and satisfying filling. Customize with your preferred toppings and enjoy the delicious flavors!

Teriyaki Tofu Stir-Fry

Ingredients:

For the Teriyaki Sauce:

- 1/4 cup soy sauce
- 2 tablespoons water
- 2 tablespoons mirin (Japanese sweet rice wine)
- 1 tablespoon rice vinegar
- 1 tablespoon brown sugar
- 1 teaspoon sesame oil
- 1 teaspoon grated ginger
- 1 teaspoon minced garlic
- 1 tablespoon cornstarch (optional, for thickening)

For the Stir-Fry:

- 14 oz (400g) firm or extra-firm tofu, pressed and cubed
- 2 tablespoons vegetable oil
- 1 bell pepper, thinly sliced (any color)
- 1 carrot, julienned
- 1 cup broccoli florets
- 1 cup snap peas, ends trimmed
- Cooked rice or noodles, for serving
- Sesame seeds and green onions, for garnish

Instructions:

Prepare Teriyaki Sauce:
- In a bowl, whisk together soy sauce, water, mirin, rice vinegar, brown sugar, sesame oil, grated ginger, and minced garlic. If you prefer a thicker sauce, mix in cornstarch dissolved in a tablespoon of water. Set aside.

Press and Cube Tofu:
- Press the tofu to remove excess water by wrapping it in a kitchen towel and placing a heavy object (like a skillet) on top for 15-20 minutes. Once pressed, cube the tofu.

Sauté Tofu:
- Heat vegetable oil in a large skillet or wok over medium-high heat. Add the cubed tofu and cook until golden brown on all sides. Remove tofu from the skillet and set aside.

Stir-Fry Vegetables:
- In the same skillet, add a bit more oil if needed. Stir-fry the bell pepper, carrot, broccoli, and snap peas until they are tender-crisp but still vibrant in color.

Combine Tofu and Vegetables:
- Add the cooked tofu back to the skillet with the vegetables.

Add Teriyaki Sauce:
- Pour the teriyaki sauce over the tofu and vegetables. Stir to coat evenly and cook for an additional 2-3 minutes until everything is heated through.

Serve:
- Serve the Teriyaki Tofu Stir-Fry over cooked rice or noodles. Garnish with sesame seeds and chopped green onions.

Enjoy this Teriyaki Tofu Stir-Fry as a tasty and nutritious plant-based meal. The teriyaki sauce adds a perfect balance of sweet and savory flavors, making this dish a satisfying and flavorful option.

Crispy Baked Lemon Garlic Chicken Thighs

Ingredients:

- 4-6 chicken thighs, bone-in, skin-on
- 2 tablespoons olive oil
- 4 cloves garlic, minced
- Zest of 1 lemon
- Juice of 1 lemon
- 1 teaspoon dried thyme
- 1 teaspoon dried rosemary
- 1 teaspoon paprika
- Salt and black pepper, to taste
- Fresh parsley, chopped, for garnish

Instructions:

Preheat Oven:
- Preheat your oven to 425°F (220°C). Line a baking sheet with parchment paper or lightly grease it.

Prepare Chicken Thighs:
- Pat the chicken thighs dry with paper towels. Place them on the prepared baking sheet.

Season Chicken:
- In a small bowl, mix together olive oil, minced garlic, lemon zest, lemon juice, dried thyme, dried rosemary, paprika, salt, and black pepper.

Coat Chicken:
- Brush the chicken thighs with the lemon-garlic mixture, ensuring they are well coated on all sides.

Bake:
- Bake in the preheated oven for 35-40 minutes or until the chicken thighs reach an internal temperature of 165°F (74°C) and the skin is crispy.

Broil for Crispiness (Optional):
- If you desire extra crispiness, you can turn on the broiler for the last 2-3 minutes of cooking, but keep a close eye to prevent burning.

Garnish and Serve:
- Remove the chicken thighs from the oven, garnish with chopped fresh parsley, and let them rest for a few minutes before serving.

Serve:

- Serve the Crispy Baked Lemon Garlic Chicken Thighs with your favorite side dishes, such as roasted vegetables, mashed potatoes, or a green salad.

This recipe delivers juicy and flavorful chicken thighs with a crispy skin thanks to the lemon and garlic-infused olive oil. It's a simple and versatile dish that pairs well with a variety of sides. Enjoy the deliciousness of this easy baked chicken recipe!

Shrimp Scampi with Linguine

Ingredients:

- 8 oz (225g) linguine pasta
- 1 lb (450g) large shrimp, peeled and deveined
- Salt and black pepper, to taste
- 3 tablespoons unsalted butter
- 3 tablespoons olive oil
- 4 cloves garlic, minced
- 1/2 teaspoon red pepper flakes (optional)
- 1/2 cup dry white wine
- Juice of 1 lemon
- Zest of 1 lemon
- 1/4 cup fresh parsley, chopped
- Grated Parmesan cheese, for serving

Instructions:

Cook Linguine:
- Cook the linguine pasta according to the package instructions in a large pot of salted boiling water. Drain and set aside.

Season Shrimp:
- Pat the shrimp dry with paper towels. Season with salt and black pepper.

Sauté Shrimp:
- In a large skillet, heat 2 tablespoons of butter and 2 tablespoons of olive oil over medium-high heat. Add the seasoned shrimp and cook for 1-2 minutes per side until they turn pink and opaque. Remove the shrimp from the skillet and set aside.

Make Sauce:
- In the same skillet, add the remaining butter and olive oil. Add minced garlic and red pepper flakes (if using) and sauté for about 1 minute until the garlic becomes fragrant. Be careful not to burn the garlic.

Deglaze with Wine:
- Pour in the dry white wine to deglaze the skillet, scraping up any browned bits from the bottom. Let it simmer for 2-3 minutes to reduce and concentrate the flavors.

Add Lemon Juice and Zest:
- Stir in the lemon juice and lemon zest, allowing the flavors to meld for another minute.

Combine Shrimp and Pasta:
- Return the cooked shrimp to the skillet. Add the drained linguine and toss everything together until the shrimp and pasta are well coated with the sauce.

Finish and Garnish:
- Sprinkle chopped fresh parsley over the shrimp and linguine. Toss once more to combine.

Serve:
- Serve the Shrimp Scampi with Linguine immediately, garnished with grated Parmesan cheese.

This Shrimp Scampi with Linguine is a delightful and quick-to-make dish that showcases the bright flavors of garlic, lemon, and white wine. It's perfect for a special dinner or any time you crave a taste of Italian cuisine. Enjoy!

Tomato Basil Grilled Cheese Sandwiches

Ingredients:

- 8 slices of bread (white, whole wheat, or your choice)
- Butter, softened
- 8 slices of your favorite cheese (cheddar, mozzarella, Swiss, etc.)
- 2 large tomatoes, thinly sliced
- Fresh basil leaves
- Salt and black pepper, to taste

Instructions:

Prepare Ingredients:
- Thinly slice the tomatoes and wash the fresh basil leaves.

Butter the Bread:
- Lay out the slices of bread and spread a thin layer of softened butter on one side of each slice.

Assemble Sandwiches:
- On the non-buttered side of half the slices, place a slice of cheese. Add a layer of thinly sliced tomatoes on top of the cheese, and then layer fresh basil leaves. Season with a pinch of salt and black pepper. Top with another slice of cheese.

Top with Bread:
- Place the remaining slices of bread on top, buttered side facing out.

Grill the Sandwiches:
- Heat a skillet or griddle over medium heat. Place the assembled sandwiches on the hot surface.

Cook until Golden:
- Cook each side for 3-4 minutes or until the bread is golden brown, and the cheese is melted.

Serve:
- Remove the Tomato Basil Grilled Cheese Sandwiches from the skillet. Allow them to cool for a minute or two before slicing. Serve warm and enjoy!

These Tomato Basil Grilled Cheese Sandwiches are a delightful twist on the classic grilled cheese. The combination of ripe tomatoes and fragrant basil adds freshness and flavor, making it a perfect choice for a quick and satisfying meal.

Lemon Herb Quinoa Salad

Ingredients:

For the Quinoa Salad:

- 1 cup quinoa, rinsed
- 2 cups water or vegetable broth
- 1 cucumber, diced
- 1 bell pepper (any color), diced
- 1 cup cherry tomatoes, halved
- 1/4 cup red onion, finely chopped
- 1/4 cup fresh parsley, chopped
- 1/4 cup fresh mint, chopped (optional)
- Feta cheese, crumbled (optional)
- Salt and black pepper, to taste

For the Lemon Herb Dressing:

- 1/4 cup extra-virgin olive oil
- Zest and juice of 2 lemons
- 1 clove garlic, minced
- 1 teaspoon Dijon mustard
- 1 teaspoon honey or maple syrup (optional)
- Salt and black pepper, to taste

Instructions:

Cook Quinoa:
- In a medium saucepan, combine quinoa and water or vegetable broth. Bring to a boil, then reduce heat to low, cover, and simmer for 15-20 minutes, or until the quinoa is cooked and water is absorbed. Fluff the quinoa with a fork and let it cool.

Prepare Vegetables:
- While the quinoa is cooking, prepare the vegetables. Dice the cucumber, bell pepper, cherry tomatoes, red onion, and chop the fresh herbs.

Make Lemon Herb Dressing:
- In a small bowl, whisk together the extra-virgin olive oil, lemon zest, lemon juice, minced garlic, Dijon mustard, honey or maple syrup (if using), salt, and black pepper. Adjust the seasoning to taste.

Combine Ingredients:
- In a large mixing bowl, combine the cooked and cooled quinoa with the diced vegetables and chopped herbs. Mix well.

Add Dressing:
- Pour the Lemon Herb Dressing over the quinoa salad. Toss everything together until well coated.

Adjust Seasoning:
- Taste the salad and adjust the seasoning if needed. Add more salt, pepper, or lemon juice according to your preferences.

Add Feta (Optional):
- If desired, crumble feta cheese over the top of the salad and gently toss.

Chill and Serve:
- Refrigerate the Lemon Herb Quinoa Salad for at least 30 minutes to let the flavors meld. Serve chilled and enjoy!

This Lemon Herb Quinoa Salad is perfect for a light and refreshing meal, as a side dish, or as a make-ahead option for picnics and gatherings. The combination of citrusy lemon, fresh herbs, and colorful vegetables makes it a flavorful and wholesome dish.

BBQ Chicken Salad with Avocado

Ingredients:

For the BBQ Chicken:

- 2 boneless, skinless chicken breasts
- Salt and black pepper, to taste
- 1 cup barbecue sauce

For the Salad:

- 6 cups mixed salad greens (e.g., lettuce, spinach, arugula)
- 1 cup cherry tomatoes, halved
- 1 cucumber, sliced
- 1 cup corn kernels (fresh, canned, or thawed frozen)
- 1/2 red onion, thinly sliced
- 1 avocado, sliced
- 1/4 cup fresh cilantro, chopped (optional)

For the BBQ Dressing:

- 1/2 cup barbecue sauce
- 2 tablespoons olive oil
- 2 tablespoons apple cider vinegar
- 1 tablespoon honey or maple syrup
- 1 teaspoon Dijon mustard
- Salt and black pepper, to taste

Instructions:

Grill Chicken:
- Season the chicken breasts with salt and black pepper. Grill the chicken over medium-high heat until fully cooked, basting with barbecue sauce during the last few minutes of grilling. Let the chicken rest for a few minutes before slicing.

Prepare Salad:
- In a large bowl, combine the mixed salad greens, cherry tomatoes, cucumber, corn, red onion, and sliced avocado.

Make BBQ Dressing:

- In a small bowl, whisk together barbecue sauce, olive oil, apple cider vinegar, honey or maple syrup, Dijon mustard, salt, and black pepper. Adjust the sweetness and acidity to taste.

Slice Chicken:
- Slice the grilled chicken breasts into thin strips.

Assemble Salad:
- Add the sliced chicken to the salad. Drizzle the BBQ dressing over the salad and toss everything together until well coated.

Garnish and Serve:
- Garnish the BBQ Chicken Salad with fresh cilantro (if using). Serve immediately.

This BBQ Chicken Salad with Avocado is a perfect blend of smoky grilled chicken, crisp vegetables, creamy avocado, and a tangy barbecue dressing. It's a hearty and flavorful salad that can be enjoyed as a light meal on its own or as a side dish for a barbecue or picnic.

Crispy Fish Tacos with Cabbage Slaw

Ingredients:

For the Crispy Fish:

- 1 lb (450g) white fish fillets (such as cod or tilapia)
- 1 cup all-purpose flour
- 1 teaspoon baking powder
- 1 teaspoon smoked paprika
- 1/2 teaspoon garlic powder
- 1/2 teaspoon onion powder
- 1/2 teaspoon salt
- 1/4 teaspoon black pepper
- 1 cup cold sparkling water (or beer)
- Vegetable oil for frying

For the Cabbage Slaw:

- 2 cups shredded green cabbage
- 1/2 cup shredded purple cabbage (optional for color)
- 1/4 cup chopped fresh cilantro
- 1/4 cup mayonnaise
- 2 tablespoons plain Greek yogurt or sour cream
- 1 tablespoon apple cider vinegar
- 1 tablespoon honey or maple syrup
- Salt and black pepper, to taste

For Serving:

- Corn tortillas
- Sliced radishes
- Lime wedges
- Hot sauce (optional)

Instructions:

Prepare Cabbage Slaw:
- In a bowl, mix together shredded green cabbage, optional purple cabbage, chopped cilantro, mayonnaise, Greek yogurt or sour cream, apple cider vinegar, honey or maple syrup, salt, and black pepper. Toss to combine. Refrigerate until ready to use.

Prepare Crispy Fish Batter:
- In a large bowl, whisk together flour, baking powder, smoked paprika, garlic powder, onion powder, salt, and black pepper. Gradually whisk in the cold sparkling water (or beer) until the batter is smooth.

Heat Oil for Frying:
- In a deep skillet or frying pan, heat vegetable oil over medium-high heat until it reaches 350°F (180°C).

Coat Fish Fillets:
- Dip each fish fillet into the batter, allowing excess batter to drip off. Carefully place the battered fillets into the hot oil.

Fry Fish:
- Fry the fish fillets for 3-4 minutes per side or until golden brown and crispy. Use a slotted spoon to transfer the crispy fish to a plate lined with paper towels to absorb excess oil.

Warm Tortillas:
- Heat corn tortillas according to package instructions.

Assemble Tacos:
- Place a crispy fish fillet on each warm tortilla. Top with a generous portion of cabbage slaw. Add sliced radishes, a squeeze of lime juice, and hot sauce if desired.

Serve:
- Serve the Crispy Fish Tacos immediately, garnished with extra cilantro if desired.

These Crispy Fish Tacos with Cabbage Slaw are a delightful combination of textures and flavors. The crispy fish pairs perfectly with the fresh and tangy cabbage slaw, creating a delicious and satisfying taco experience. Enjoy!

Pesto Zoodle Bowl with Grilled Chicken

Ingredients:

For the Pesto Sauce:

- 2 cups fresh basil leaves, packed
- 1/2 cup grated Parmesan cheese
- 1/3 cup pine nuts or walnuts
- 2 cloves garlic, minced
- 1/2 cup extra-virgin olive oil
- Salt and black pepper, to taste
- Juice of 1 lemon

For the Zoodle Bowl:

- 4 medium-sized zucchinis, spiralized into noodles
- 1 tablespoon olive oil
- 4 boneless, skinless chicken breasts
- Salt and black pepper, to taste
- Lemon wedges, for serving
- Optional toppings: cherry tomatoes, sliced olives, grated Parmesan

Instructions:

For the Pesto Sauce:

Prepare Pesto:
- In a food processor, combine basil, Parmesan cheese, pine nuts or walnuts, and minced garlic. Pulse until coarsely chopped.

Add Olive Oil:
- With the food processor running, slowly pour in the olive oil in a steady stream until the pesto reaches your desired consistency.

Season and Finish:
- Season the pesto with salt and black pepper to taste. Add lemon juice and pulse to combine. Adjust seasoning if needed.

For the Zoodle Bowl:

Prepare Zoodles:
- Spiralize the zucchinis into noodles using a spiralizer. Set aside.

Grill Chicken:

- Preheat the grill or grill pan over medium-high heat. Season the chicken breasts with salt and black pepper. Grill the chicken for about 6-8 minutes per side or until fully cooked.

Cook Zoodles:
- In a large skillet, heat olive oil over medium heat. Add the zucchini noodles and sauté for 2-3 minutes until they are just tender but still have a bit of crunch.

Toss with Pesto:
- Add a generous amount of pesto to the zucchini noodles and toss to coat evenly.

Slice Chicken:
- Slice the grilled chicken breasts into thin strips.

Assemble Bowls:
- Divide the pesto-coated zucchini noodles among serving bowls. Top with grilled chicken slices. Add optional toppings like cherry tomatoes, sliced olives, and grated Parmesan if desired.

Serve:
- Serve the Pesto Zoodle Bowl with Grilled Chicken immediately, garnished with lemon wedges on the side.

This Pesto Zoodle Bowl with Grilled Chicken is a low-carb and nutrient-packed dish that is bursting with fresh flavors. It's a perfect meal for a light lunch or dinner, especially during warmer seasons. Enjoy!

Mongolian Beef Skillet

Ingredients:

- 1 lb (450g) flank steak, thinly sliced against the grain
- 1/4 cup cornstarch
- 2 tablespoons vegetable oil
- 3 cloves garlic, minced
- 1 teaspoon fresh ginger, grated
- 1/2 cup low-sodium soy sauce
- 1/2 cup water
- 1/2 cup brown sugar, packed
- 2 tablespoons hoisin sauce
- 1 tablespoon rice vinegar
- 1/2 teaspoon red pepper flakes (optional)
- 2 green onions, sliced (for garnish)
- Sesame seeds (for garnish)
- Cooked rice or noodles, for serving

Instructions:

Coat Beef:
- In a bowl, toss the thinly sliced flank steak with cornstarch until well coated.

Sear Beef:
- Heat vegetable oil in a large skillet or wok over medium-high heat. Add the coated beef slices and sear until browned on all sides. Remove the beef from the skillet and set aside.

Sauté Aromatics:
- In the same skillet, add minced garlic and grated ginger. Sauté for about 1 minute until fragrant.

Make Sauce:
- In a bowl, whisk together soy sauce, water, brown sugar, hoisin sauce, rice vinegar, and red pepper flakes if using.

Simmer Sauce:
- Pour the sauce mixture into the skillet with the garlic and ginger. Bring to a simmer and let it cook for 2-3 minutes, allowing the sauce to thicken slightly.

Add Beef Back:

- Return the seared beef to the skillet, tossing to coat the beef slices evenly with the sauce. Cook for an additional 2-3 minutes until the beef is heated through.

Garnish and Serve:
- Garnish the Mongolian Beef Skillet with sliced green onions and sesame seeds.

Serve:
- Serve the Mongolian Beef over cooked rice or noodles.

This Mongolian Beef Skillet is a delicious and speedy way to enjoy the flavors of a classic takeout dish at home. The savory and sweet sauce complements the tender beef, creating a satisfying meal that's perfect for busy weeknights. Enjoy!

Caprese Stuffed Chicken Breast

Ingredients:

- 4 boneless, skinless chicken breasts
- Salt and black pepper, to taste
- 1 teaspoon Italian seasoning
- 4 ounces fresh mozzarella cheese, sliced
- 2 large tomatoes, sliced
- Fresh basil leaves
- Balsamic glaze, for drizzling
- Olive oil, for brushing
- Toothpicks or kitchen twine

Instructions:

Preheat Oven:
- Preheat your oven to 400°F (200°C).

Prepare Chicken:
- Place each chicken breast between sheets of plastic wrap and gently pound to an even thickness (about 1/2 inch). Season each side with salt, black pepper, and Italian seasoning.

Layer Caprese Filling:
- On one side of each chicken breast, layer slices of fresh mozzarella, tomato, and fresh basil leaves.

Fold and Secure:
- Carefully fold the other side of the chicken breast over the filling, creating a stuffed chicken breast. Secure the edges with toothpicks or tie with kitchen twine to hold the filling in place.

Brush with Olive Oil:
- Brush the outside of each stuffed chicken breast with olive oil.

Sear Chicken:
- Heat an oven-safe skillet over medium-high heat. Sear each stuffed chicken breast for 2-3 minutes on each side until golden brown.

Finish in the Oven:
- Transfer the skillet to the preheated oven and bake for 20-25 minutes or until the chicken is cooked through and reaches an internal temperature of 165°F (74°C).

Drizzle with Balsamic Glaze:

- Remove the stuffed chicken breasts from the oven. Drizzle with balsamic glaze for added flavor.

Serve:
- Serve the Caprese Stuffed Chicken Breast warm, garnished with additional fresh basil if desired.

This Caprese Stuffed Chicken Breast is a flavorful and elegant dish that's perfect for a special dinner or when you want to impress with a restaurant-style meal at home. The combination of mozzarella, tomatoes, and fresh basil creates a burst of Mediterranean flavors. Enjoy!

Quick and Easy Margherita Pasta

Ingredients:

- 8 ounces (225g) spaghetti or your favorite pasta
- 2 tablespoons olive oil
- 3 cloves garlic, minced
- 1 pint (about 2 cups) cherry or grape tomatoes, halved
- Salt and black pepper, to taste
- Crushed red pepper flakes, to taste (optional)
- Fresh mozzarella balls or torn fresh mozzarella
- Fresh basil leaves, torn or chopped
- Grated Parmesan cheese, for serving

Instructions:

Cook Pasta:
- Cook the pasta according to the package instructions in a large pot of salted boiling water. Drain and set aside.

Sauté Garlic and Tomatoes:
- In a large skillet, heat olive oil over medium heat. Add minced garlic and sauté for about 1 minute until fragrant. Add the halved cherry tomatoes to the skillet.

Season and Cook Tomatoes:
- Season the tomatoes with salt, black pepper, and optional crushed red pepper flakes. Cook for 5-7 minutes, stirring occasionally, until the tomatoes soften and release their juices.

Combine Pasta and Tomatoes:
- Add the cooked and drained pasta to the skillet with the tomatoes. Toss everything together until the pasta is well coated with the tomato mixture.

Add Mozzarella and Basil:
- Add fresh mozzarella balls or torn mozzarella to the pasta, allowing it to melt slightly. Add torn or chopped fresh basil leaves.

Serve:
- Serve the Margherita Pasta warm, garnished with additional fresh basil and grated Parmesan cheese.

This Quick and Easy Margherita Pasta is a light and flavorful dish that captures the essence of the classic Margherita pizza. The combination of sweet cherry tomatoes, fresh mozzarella, and aromatic basil creates a simple yet satisfying pasta dish. Enjoy!

Lemon Dill Salmon Cakes

Ingredients:

- 2 cans (14 ounces each) canned salmon, drained
- 1/2 cup breadcrumbs
- 1/4 cup mayonnaise
- 1 large egg
- 2 tablespoons Dijon mustard
- 2 tablespoons fresh lemon juice
- 1 tablespoon fresh dill, chopped
- 1 teaspoon lemon zest
- Salt and black pepper, to taste
- Olive oil, for cooking

Instructions:

Prepare Salmon Mixture:
- In a large mixing bowl, combine the drained canned salmon, breadcrumbs, mayonnaise, egg, Dijon mustard, fresh lemon juice, chopped dill, lemon zest, salt, and black pepper.

Mix Ingredients:
- Mix the ingredients together until well combined. The mixture should hold together when shaped into patties. If it's too wet, you can add more breadcrumbs.

Form Salmon Cakes:
- Divide the salmon mixture into equal portions and shape them into patties.

Chill in the Refrigerator:
- Place the salmon patties in the refrigerator for at least 30 minutes. This helps them firm up and hold their shape during cooking.

Cook Salmon Cakes:
- Heat olive oil in a skillet over medium heat. Cook the salmon cakes for about 4-5 minutes per side or until they are golden brown and cooked through.

Serve:
- Serve the Lemon Dill Salmon Cakes warm. They pair well with a side salad, a squeeze of lemon juice, or a dollop of tartar sauce.

Enjoy these Lemon Dill Salmon Cakes as a light and flavorful meal. The combination of lemon and dill adds a refreshing twist to the savory salmon cakes.

Mushroom and Goat Cheese Omelette

Ingredients:

- 3 large eggs
- Salt and black pepper, to taste
- 1 tablespoon butter or olive oil
- 1 cup mushrooms, sliced
- 2 ounces goat cheese, crumbled
- Fresh chives, chopped (for garnish, optional)

Instructions:

    Prepare Eggs:
- Crack the eggs into a bowl, season with salt and black pepper, and beat them with a fork or whisk until well combined.

    Sauté Mushrooms:
- In a non-stick skillet, heat butter or olive oil over medium heat. Add the sliced mushrooms and sauté for 3-4 minutes until they are tender and any released liquid has evaporated. Season with a pinch of salt.

    Cook Eggs:
- Pour the beaten eggs into the skillet over the sautéed mushrooms. Allow the eggs to set slightly at the edges.

    Add Goat Cheese:
- Sprinkle crumbled goat cheese over one half of the omelette.

    Fold and Serve:
- Once the edges are set and the center is still slightly runny, carefully fold the omelette in half using a spatula.

    Finish Cooking:
- Cook for an additional 1-2 minutes until the eggs are fully cooked but still moist.

    Garnish and Serve:
- Slide the Mushroom and Goat Cheese Omelette onto a plate. Garnish with fresh chives if desired.

Enjoy your Mushroom and Goat Cheese Omelette as a satisfying and flavorful breakfast. The earthy mushrooms and creamy goat cheese create a delightful combination in each bite.

Sesame Orange Chicken Lettuce Wraps

Ingredients:

For the Sesame Orange Chicken:

- 1 lb (450g) boneless, skinless chicken breasts, diced
- Salt and black pepper, to taste
- 2 tablespoons vegetable oil
- 1/2 cup orange juice
- 1/4 cup soy sauce
- 3 tablespoons honey
- 2 tablespoons rice vinegar
- 2 cloves garlic, minced
- 1 teaspoon grated fresh ginger
- 1 tablespoon cornstarch mixed with 2 tablespoons water
- Sesame seeds, for garnish

For the Lettuce Wraps:

- Iceberg or butter lettuce leaves, washed and separated
- Shredded carrots
- Sliced green onions
- Chopped cilantro (optional)
- Crushed red pepper flakes (optional)

Instructions:

For the Sesame Orange Chicken:

Season Chicken:
- Season diced chicken with salt and black pepper.

Sear Chicken:
- Heat vegetable oil in a large skillet over medium-high heat. Sear the chicken until browned on all sides and cooked through.

Make Sauce:
- In a small bowl, whisk together orange juice, soy sauce, honey, rice vinegar, minced garlic, and grated ginger.

Combine and Thicken:
- Pour the sauce mixture over the cooked chicken. Stir in the cornstarch-water mixture. Cook until the sauce thickens.

Garnish:
- Garnish with sesame seeds and set aside.

For the Lettuce Wraps:

Prepare Lettuce Leaves:
- Wash and separate the lettuce leaves. Pat them dry with paper towels.

Assemble Wraps:
- Spoon the Sesame Orange Chicken into each lettuce leaf.

Add Toppings:
- Top with shredded carrots, sliced green onions, and chopped cilantro if desired.

Optional Garnish:
- Sprinkle with crushed red pepper flakes for a bit of heat.

Serve:
- Serve the Sesame Orange Chicken Lettuce Wraps immediately.

These Sesame Orange Chicken Lettuce Wraps are a delicious combination of sweet and savory flavors with a refreshing crunch from the lettuce. They make for a light and satisfying meal or appetizer. Enjoy!

Crispy Chickpea and Avocado Wrap

Ingredients:

For the Crispy Chickpeas:

- 1 can (15 ounces) chickpeas, drained and rinsed
- 1 tablespoon olive oil
- 1 teaspoon ground cumin
- 1 teaspoon smoked paprika
- Salt and black pepper, to taste

For the Wrap:

- Whole-grain or spinach tortillas
- Romaine lettuce leaves
- 1 large avocado, sliced
- Cherry tomatoes, halved
- Red onion, thinly sliced
- Greek yogurt or tzatziki sauce for drizzling
- Fresh cilantro or parsley, chopped (optional)

Instructions:

For the Crispy Chickpeas:

   Preheat Oven:
   - Preheat your oven to 400°F (200°C).

   Dry Chickpeas:
   - Pat the drained chickpeas dry with a paper towel to remove excess moisture.

   Season Chickpeas:
   - In a bowl, toss the chickpeas with olive oil, ground cumin, smoked paprika, salt, and black pepper.

   Bake Chickpeas:
   - Spread the seasoned chickpeas in a single layer on a baking sheet. Bake in the preheated oven for 20-25 minutes or until they become crispy, shaking the pan occasionally for even cooking.

Assembling the Wrap:

Prepare Ingredients:
- While the chickpeas are baking, prepare the wrap ingredients: slice the avocado, halve the cherry tomatoes, and thinly slice the red onion.

Warm Tortillas:
- If desired, warm the tortillas in a dry skillet for a few seconds on each side.

Assemble Wrap:
- Lay a tortilla flat and layer with Romaine lettuce leaves. Add a portion of the crispy chickpeas, sliced avocado, cherry tomatoes, and red onion.

Drizzle Sauce:
- Drizzle Greek yogurt or tzatziki sauce over the ingredients.

Garnish:
- Garnish with fresh cilantro or parsley if desired.

Wrap and Serve:
- Fold the sides of the tortilla and roll it up tightly to form the wrap. Cut in half diagonally if preferred.

Serve:
- Serve the Crispy Chickpea and Avocado Wrap immediately.

This Crispy Chickpea and Avocado Wrap is a flavorful and satisfying meal that combines the crunch of the chickpeas with the creamy texture of avocado. It's a great option for a quick and healthy lunch or dinner. Enjoy!

Shrimp and Broccoli Alfredo

Ingredients:

- 8 ounces fettuccine pasta
- 1 pound large shrimp, peeled and deveined
- Salt and black pepper, to taste
- 2 tablespoons olive oil
- 3 cloves garlic, minced
- 1 cup broccoli florets, blanched
- 1 cup heavy cream
- 1 cup grated Parmesan cheese
- 1/2 cup unsalted butter
- 1 teaspoon garlic powder
- 1 teaspoon onion powder
- 1/2 teaspoon nutmeg (optional)
- Fresh parsley, chopped (for garnish)

Instructions:

Cook Fettuccine:
- Cook the fettuccine pasta according to the package instructions in a large pot of salted boiling water. Drain and set aside.

Season and Cook Shrimp:
- Season the shrimp with salt and black pepper. In a large skillet, heat olive oil over medium-high heat. Add minced garlic and cook until fragrant. Add the shrimp and cook for 2-3 minutes per side until they turn pink. Remove the shrimp from the skillet and set aside.

Prepare Alfredo Sauce:
- In the same skillet, melt butter over medium heat. Stir in heavy cream, garlic powder, onion powder, and nutmeg (if using). Bring the mixture to a simmer.

Add Parmesan Cheese:
- Reduce the heat to low and gradually whisk in the grated Parmesan cheese until the sauce is smooth and creamy.

Combine Pasta, Shrimp, and Broccoli:
- Add the cooked fettuccine pasta, cooked shrimp, and blanched broccoli to the Alfredo sauce. Toss everything together until well coated in the sauce.

Adjust Seasoning:
- Season with additional salt and black pepper to taste.

Garnish and Serve:
- Garnish with chopped fresh parsley and serve the Shrimp and Broccoli Alfredo warm.

This Shrimp and Broccoli Alfredo is a rich and satisfying pasta dish that combines succulent shrimp, crisp broccoli, and a creamy Alfredo sauce. It's perfect for a special dinner or when you're craving a comforting meal. Enjoy!

Southwest Quinoa Bowl

Ingredients:

For the Quinoa Bowl:

- 1 cup quinoa, rinsed
- 2 cups water or vegetable broth
- 1 can (15 ounces) black beans, drained and rinsed
- 1 cup corn kernels (fresh, frozen, or canned)
- 1 cup cherry tomatoes, halved
- 1 avocado, diced
- 1/2 cup red onion, finely chopped
- Fresh cilantro, chopped (for garnish)
- Lime wedges (for serving)

For the Southwest Dressing:

- 1/4 cup olive oil
- 2 tablespoons lime juice
- 1 teaspoon ground cumin
- 1 teaspoon chili powder
- 1/2 teaspoon garlic powder
- Salt and black pepper, to taste

Instructions:

For the Quinoa Bowl:

Cook Quinoa:
- In a medium saucepan, combine quinoa and water or vegetable broth. Bring to a boil, then reduce heat to low, cover, and simmer for 15-20 minutes or until quinoa is cooked and water is absorbed. Fluff quinoa with a fork.

Assemble Bowl:
- In serving bowls, layer cooked quinoa with black beans, corn, cherry tomatoes, diced avocado, and chopped red onion.

For the Southwest Dressing:

Prepare Dressing:
- In a small bowl, whisk together olive oil, lime juice, ground cumin, chili powder, garlic powder, salt, and black pepper.

Drizzle Dressing:
- Drizzle the Southwest dressing over the assembled quinoa bowls.

Garnish and Serve:
- Garnish with chopped fresh cilantro and serve the Southwest Quinoa Bowls with lime wedges on the side.

This Southwest Quinoa Bowl is a vibrant and satisfying dish that brings together the flavors of quinoa, black beans, corn, avocado, and a zesty Southwest dressing. It's a versatile and customizable recipe that you can adapt to your taste preferences. Enjoy!

Sheet Pan Fajitas with Chicken

Ingredients:

For the Chicken and Vegetables:

- 1.5 lbs (about 700g) boneless, skinless chicken breasts, thinly sliced
- 3 bell peppers (assorted colors), thinly sliced
- 1 large red onion, thinly sliced
- 3 tablespoons olive oil
- 1 tablespoon chili powder
- 1 teaspoon ground cumin
- 1 teaspoon smoked paprika
- 1 teaspoon garlic powder
- 1 teaspoon onion powder
- 1/2 teaspoon cayenne pepper (optional, for extra heat)
- Salt and black pepper, to taste

For Serving:

- Flour tortillas
- Lime wedges
- Fresh cilantro, chopped
- Sour cream or Greek yogurt
- Salsa

Instructions:

Preheat Oven:
- Preheat your oven to 400°F (200°C).

Prepare Chicken and Vegetables:
- In a large bowl, combine the sliced chicken, bell peppers, and red onion. Drizzle with olive oil and sprinkle with chili powder, ground cumin, smoked paprika, garlic powder, onion powder, cayenne pepper (if using), salt, and black pepper. Toss until well coated.

Arrange on Sheet Pan:
- Spread the seasoned chicken and vegetables on a large sheet pan in a single layer.

Bake:

- Bake in the preheated oven for 20-25 minutes or until the chicken is cooked through and the vegetables are tender. You can stir or flip the ingredients halfway through cooking for even browning.

Warm Tortillas:
- In the last 5 minutes of baking, you can warm the flour tortillas directly on the oven rack or wrapped in aluminum foil.

Serve:
- Remove the sheet pan from the oven. Serve the sheet pan fajitas with warm tortillas and your choice of toppings, such as lime wedges, chopped cilantro, sour cream or Greek yogurt, and salsa.

These Sheet Pan Fajitas with Chicken are a hassle-free and flavorful way to enjoy a classic Tex-Mex dish. The oven does most of the work, and you can customize the toppings to suit your preferences. Enjoy!

Greek Chicken Souvlaki

Ingredients:

For the Chicken Marinade:

- 1.5 lbs (about 700g) boneless, skinless chicken breasts, cut into bite-sized pieces
- 1/4 cup olive oil
- 3 tablespoons plain Greek yogurt
- 3 cloves garlic, minced
- 1 teaspoon dried oregano
- 1 teaspoon dried thyme
- 1 teaspoon ground cumin
- Zest and juice of 1 lemon
- Salt and black pepper, to taste

For Serving:

- Pita bread or flatbreads
- Tzatziki sauce
- Cherry tomatoes, sliced cucumbers, red onion slices (optional)
- Fresh parsley, chopped (for garnish)

Instructions:

Prepare Marinade:
- In a bowl, whisk together olive oil, Greek yogurt, minced garlic, dried oregano, dried thyme, ground cumin, lemon zest, lemon juice, salt, and black pepper to create the marinade.

Marinate Chicken:
- Place the bite-sized chicken pieces in a resealable plastic bag or a shallow dish. Pour the marinade over the chicken, ensuring all pieces are well coated. Seal the bag or cover the dish and refrigerate for at least 30 minutes to marinate.

Preheat Grill:
- Preheat your grill or grill pan to medium-high heat.

Skewer Chicken:
- Thread the marinated chicken pieces onto skewers.

Grill Chicken Skewers:

- Grill the chicken skewers for 6-8 minutes, turning occasionally, until the chicken is cooked through and has a nice char.

Warm Pita Bread:
- In the last couple of minutes, warm the pita bread on the grill.

Serve:
- Serve the Greek Chicken Souvlaki on warm pita bread, accompanied by tzatziki sauce. You can also add sliced cherry tomatoes, cucumber, and red onion if desired.

Garnish:
- Garnish with chopped fresh parsley and serve immediately.

This Greek Chicken Souvlaki is a perfect balance of Mediterranean flavors, and the marinated chicken becomes tender and flavorful after grilling. Enjoy it as a wrap or in a plate with your favorite Mediterranean sides.

Cilantro Lime Shrimp Tacos

Ingredients:

For the Cilantro Lime Shrimp:

- 1 lb large shrimp, peeled and deveined
- 2 tablespoons olive oil
- 3 cloves garlic, minced
- Zest and juice of 2 limes
- 1 teaspoon ground cumin
- 1 teaspoon chili powder
- Salt and black pepper, to taste
- Fresh cilantro, chopped (for garnish)

For Serving:

- Corn or flour tortillas
- Shredded cabbage or lettuce
- Diced tomatoes
- Sliced avocado or guacamole
- Greek yogurt or sour cream
- Lime wedges

Instructions:

For the Cilantro Lime Shrimp:

Marinate Shrimp:
- In a bowl, combine shrimp with olive oil, minced garlic, lime zest, lime juice, ground cumin, chili powder, salt, and black pepper. Toss to coat the shrimp evenly. Allow it to marinate for 15-20 minutes.

Cook Shrimp:
- In a skillet over medium-high heat, cook the marinated shrimp for 2-3 minutes per side or until they turn pink and opaque.

Garnish:
- Garnish the cooked shrimp with freshly chopped cilantro.

For Serving:

Prepare Toppings:

- While the shrimp is cooking, prepare your desired toppings, such as shredded cabbage or lettuce, diced tomatoes, sliced avocado or guacamole, and lime wedges.

Warm Tortillas:
- Warm the tortillas according to package instructions.

Assemble Tacos:
- Assemble the Cilantro Lime Shrimp Tacos by placing a portion of cooked shrimp on each tortilla. Top with shredded cabbage or lettuce, diced tomatoes, sliced avocado or guacamole, and a dollop of Greek yogurt or sour cream.

Serve:
- Serve the tacos with lime wedges on the side.

These Cilantro Lime Shrimp Tacos are a burst of citrusy and herby flavors. They are quick to make and customizable with your favorite toppings. Enjoy these tacos for a refreshing and satisfying meal!

Pasta Primavera with Lemon Parmesan Sauce

Ingredients:

- 8 ounces (about 225g) pasta (linguine, fettuccine, or your choice)
- 2 tablespoons olive oil
- 3 cloves garlic, minced
- 1 cup cherry tomatoes, halved
- 1 medium zucchini, thinly sliced
- 1 medium yellow squash, thinly sliced
- 1 cup broccoli florets
- 1 bell pepper, thinly sliced (any color)
- 1/2 cup grated Parmesan cheese
- Zest and juice of 1 lemon
- Salt and black pepper, to taste
- Crushed red pepper flakes (optional, for heat)
- Fresh basil or parsley, chopped (for garnish)

Instructions:

Cook Pasta:
- Cook the pasta according to the package instructions in a large pot of salted boiling water. Drain and set aside.

Sauté Vegetables:
- In a large skillet, heat olive oil over medium heat. Add minced garlic and sauté until fragrant. Add cherry tomatoes, zucchini, yellow squash, broccoli, and bell pepper. Cook for 5-7 minutes, or until the vegetables are tender-crisp.

Prepare Lemon Parmesan Sauce:
- Stir in the grated Parmesan cheese, lemon zest, and lemon juice. Season with salt and black pepper to taste. Add crushed red pepper flakes if you like a bit of heat.

Combine Pasta and Sauce:
- Add the cooked pasta to the skillet with the lemon Parmesan sauce and toss until the pasta is well coated and the vegetables are evenly distributed.

Garnish and Serve:
- Garnish with chopped fresh basil or parsley. Serve the Pasta Primavera with Lemon Parmesan Sauce immediately.

This Pasta Primavera is a vibrant and flavorful dish that highlights the freshness of seasonal vegetables. The lemony Parmesan sauce adds a bright and zesty twist to the pasta. Enjoy this light and delicious meal!

Caprese Quinoa Salad

Ingredients:

For the Salad:

- 1 cup quinoa, rinsed
- 2 cups cherry tomatoes, halved
- 1 cup fresh mozzarella balls (bocconcini), halved
- 1/2 cup fresh basil leaves, torn
- Balsamic glaze (for drizzling)
- Salt and black pepper, to taste

For the Dressing:

- 3 tablespoons extra-virgin olive oil
- 1 tablespoon balsamic vinegar
- 1 clove garlic, minced
- Salt and black pepper, to taste

Instructions:

Cook Quinoa:
- In a medium saucepan, combine quinoa with 2 cups of water. Bring to a boil, then reduce the heat to low, cover, and simmer for 15-20 minutes or until the quinoa is cooked and water is absorbed. Fluff with a fork and let it cool.

Prepare Dressing:
- In a small bowl, whisk together extra-virgin olive oil, balsamic vinegar, minced garlic, salt, and black pepper to create the dressing.

Assemble Salad:
- In a large bowl, combine the cooked and cooled quinoa, cherry tomatoes, fresh mozzarella balls, and torn fresh basil.

Add Dressing:
- Pour the dressing over the salad and toss gently to coat all the ingredients. Season with additional salt and black pepper if needed.

Drizzle with Balsamic Glaze:
- Drizzle the Caprese Quinoa Salad with balsamic glaze for an extra burst of flavor.

Serve:

- Serve the salad immediately or refrigerate until ready to serve. It can be enjoyed chilled or at room temperature.

This Caprese Quinoa Salad is a light and satisfying dish that makes a perfect side dish or a light lunch. The combination of quinoa, tomatoes, fresh mozzarella, and basil creates a colorful and flavorful salad. Enjoy!

Quick and Easy Beef Burrito Bowl

Ingredients:

For the Beef:

- 1 lb ground beef
- 1 tablespoon olive oil
- 1 small onion, finely chopped
- 2 cloves garlic, minced
- 1 tablespoon chili powder
- 1 teaspoon ground cumin
- 1 teaspoon paprika
- Salt and black pepper, to taste

For the Rice:

- 1 cup white or brown rice
- 2 cups water or beef broth
- Salt, to taste

For Assembling:

- 1 can (15 ounces) black beans, drained and rinsed
- Corn kernels (fresh, frozen, or canned)
- Salsa or pico de gallo
- Guacamole or sliced avocado
- Shredded lettuce
- Shredded cheese
- Sour cream
- Fresh cilantro, chopped (for garnish)
- Lime wedges

Instructions:

For the Beef:

   Cook Beef:
   - In a skillet, heat olive oil over medium-high heat. Add chopped onions and minced garlic, sautéing until softened.

   Brown Beef:

- Add ground beef and cook until browned, breaking it apart with a spatula.

Season Beef:
- Sprinkle chili powder, ground cumin, paprika, salt, and black pepper over the beef. Stir to combine and cook until the beef is well seasoned and cooked through.

For the Rice:

Cook Rice:
- In a separate pot, combine rice and water or beef broth. Bring to a boil, then reduce heat to low, cover, and simmer until the rice is cooked and water is absorbed. Fluff with a fork.

For Assembling:

Assemble Bowls:
- In individual serving bowls, layer cooked rice, seasoned beef, black beans, corn, salsa or pico de gallo, guacamole or sliced avocado, shredded lettuce, and shredded cheese.

Top with Toppings:
- Garnish with sour cream, chopped cilantro, and lime wedges.

Serve:
- Serve the Quick and Easy Beef Burrito Bowls immediately, allowing everyone to customize their bowls with their favorite toppings.

This Beef Burrito Bowl is a convenient and satisfying meal that brings the flavors of a burrito in a bowl. Feel free to customize it with your preferred toppings for a delicious and hearty dinner. Enjoy!

www.ingramcontent.com/pod-product-compliance
Lightning Source LLC
LaVergne TN
LVHW081605060526
838201LV00054B/2093